MW01138309

BOWER LODGE

Paul J. Pastor

In *Bower Lodge*, Paul Pastor rejoices in language, mythic pattern, and the great transcendentals of truth and beauty. This fluent singer praises wild creation, great or small, snared in the nets of time. Above all, he is wonderfully inspired by the Mystery that brings on transformation and rebirth.

Marly Youmans
author of *Charis in the World of Wonders* and
The Book of the Red King

Paul Pastor certainly has "the poet's eye": he constantly directs your gaze at unnoticed details, overlooked beauties, luminous images. But he does more than that. Time and again, the images in this collection are transformed into metaphors, emblems, symbols: images to think with and look through so that the *Bower Lodge* itself becomes a local habitation for wisdom we might otherwise have missed.

Malcolm Guite
author of *Lifting the Veil* and *David's Crown*

Bower Lodge invites the reader into the wild and liminal places of the natural world, "unsafe, unnumb," into river, bower, hive, and toadstool, digging underground and then up again, in pursuit of "a death that feeds/ the rooted life/ in the secret kingdom." With a meticulous eye to landscapes of both woods and the soul, Pastor deftly depicts the disassembly and reassembly necessary for the flourishing of each. The poems in this sparkling debut collection do not shy away from the "common, secret grief" of the world, trusting that, like the seed, like the dry bones in Ezekiel, new life comes "up now/ skull town/ bone sound/ blooming like the true me."

Laura Reece Hogan
author of *Litany of Flights: Poems*

Paul J. Pastor shines a bodily spirit onto *Bower Lodge*. Humanity brims the soul first; then the body turns to shine, every syllable camping on hills and in valleys. The unknown graces God. His words exact every living thing—aches, maggots, dreams, encompassing the poet's truth-seeking toward a Self. Instinct survives. Desire scrambles to consume the longing body and soul harmoniously.

Shelby Stephenson
poet laureate of North Carolina, 2015-2018,
author of *Shelby's Lady: The Hog Poems*

Bower Lodge is lightning on the mountain, night fires in the deep dark, a song of abandon from the throats of wolves. Below the fierce wilderness in this collection, each poem speaks with uncommon tenderness toward that which we too often avoid... the demands of love, the heart of a friend, the beauty of the uncontainable wild, the enfolding power of death, and the fearful ascent of new life harbored in the soul of God. If the Spirit of Life is a bird, and if hope is the thing with feathers as Dickinson so truly intoned, Paul J. Pastor's poems are a kind of transcendence grounded in the earth, touched by water, while at the same time lifting toward a boundless sky of which we, in our human reality, know very little. *Bower Lodge* takes us in all our vulnerability, shapes our lives into earthen windborne vessels, and helps us ascend into a higher, deeper heaven.

Shann Ray
author of *American Masculine*,
Sweetclover, and *Atomic Theory 7*

For all its intimations of quietude, there's a wildness in Pastor's poems—think Berryman's dreaming songs or Whitman's barbarian yawp—a rusticity that is as defiant as it is pastoral. This book is a plumage, not of butterfly or bird, but of moth wing, which is to say: a blessing.

Mischa Willett
author of *The Elegy Beta* and *Phases*

In Paul Pastor's poetic vision, the timebound earth transcends time even as it marks it in seasons both natural and liturgical, with their recurrent endings and renewals. In considering "the simple things"— root and seed, "the plumage of a moth"—these poems affirm, again and again, the essential goodness of creation in what Hopkins called its inscape and its instress: its existence in all its infinite particularity and the ways that the human mind and heart receive that infinite particularity as experience. Like Hopkins', Pastor's poems seek to translate inscape into instress, to open human eyes to the whole created order, shining according to its kind with the image of God. Nature itself becomes in these poems a translation of that presence, mysterious in its doings in this world but blinding in its unfiltered intensity. "We who live in wonders/ must be blind to wonders./ If fish could see the water,/ they could see nothing else." In poem after poem, Pastor calls forth the mystery, radiant and devastating, that "hangs/ bright beyond [our] reach."

Sally Thomas
author of *Motherland*

Paul Pastor is a man who refuses to eat mahogany. In other words, the poetry in his collection *Bower Lodge* illumines not the bizarre, but the common—like irises in the sun and summer blackberries and warrens of lean hares. Far from simple, these poems demand an attention from the reader (risky). But with great risk comes great reward.

John Blase
author of *The Jubilee*

Welcome, reader, to *Bower Lodge,* a hero's journey both visceral and holy. Take the hand of the beloved Wanderer and "romp the endless/ cathedral of a raspberry," or be pulled "thrilled, protesting, gooped and bloody at the gills,/ into the air." These gorgeous poems are wrested from fir-shadows and jars of salt; they partake in creaturely communion with spider and fly. Here Paul Pastor speaks from the sounding depths. And he is a poet to rely on, as we might a wilderness guide who possesses secret knowledge of backcountry routes and highly potent natural cures. Enter here, into "the rizz and raggle of my laden thought," and cross over to an enlarged and exhilarated consciousness, into mythic and numinous territory, into Meaning and Being.

Leslie Williams
author of *Even the Dark* and *Success of the Seed Plants*

This isn't a book. It's a wondrous house full of visions and stories and half-remembered dreams. We've been here before, we realize, but somehow forgotten everything, even our true names. When Paul Pastor opens the door and welcomes us in, let's stay.

Sarah Arthur
author of *Light Upon Light: A Literary Guide to Prayer for Advent,
Christmas, and Epiphany*

A lyrical light-footedness moves the wisdom of *Bower Lodge* forward. Paul Pastor's book never neglects to delight us even as it burrows deeper into the bower, like a game of hide and seek. "Name it, I dare you, before the breeze shifts," the speaker tells us, and despite their heady wealth, the language of these poems leaps clear of exposition "before the palate is cleaned by too much thought." Pastor has woven a collection of reverent lifesongs musical enough to avoid didacticism and yet accessible enough for readers to hum along.

Justin Rigamonti
managing director of Poetry Press Week

With a faultless ear, steady line, and a Whitmanesque *joie de vivre*, Pastor's kindness is always one step ahead of us as he leads through the environs of the imagination. And we need a guide because, as he reminds us "we who live in wonders/ must be blind to wonders."

Dan Rattelle
author of *The Commonwealth*

With a cinematographer's eye for precise images ("owl pellets sopped in dew," "morning glories tendril brown iron"), and a safecracker's ear for rhythm and music, Pastor's finely-wrought poems seek out the sorrows and beauty of our world—and the mortal shine behind that beauty—in a search for language we do not yet have. Pastor always has one tailfeather fixed on the spiritual—and the eternal—and in these poems "beauty wets her beak and coughs a bone," a poetry that plumbs the world within our world, and the one beyond it. When Pastor discovers joy, it is a fierce and authentic and hard-won joy indeed.

Mark Wagenaar
author of *Southern Tongues Leave Us Shining*

BOWER LODGE

Poems

Paul J. Pastor

Fernwood
PRESS

Bower Lodge

poems

©2021 by Paul J. Pastor

Fernwood Press
Newberg, Oregon
www.fernwoodpress.com

All rights reserved. No part may be reproduced
for any commercial purpose by any method without
permission in writing from the copyright holder.

Printed in the United States of America

Page design: Mareesa Fawver Moss

Cover art and illustrations: Jacob Cowdin

Author photo: Mark Pratt-Russum

ISBN 978-1-59498-074-9

Library of Congress Control Number: 2021950493

"Benediction" was first published by *The Windhover.*
"The Roof Slants, So the Water Pours This Way "and "The Tearing
    of the Green" were first published by *Fathom.*
"Her Dusking Avenues" was first published and anthologized by
    The New York Quarterly Review in *Without a Doubt: Poems Illuminating
    Faith.*
"The Raspberry Kid" was first published by *Ekstasis.*
"Ephesus at Sunset," "Telemachus Among the Suitors," and "The
    Mustness" were first published by Solum Literary Press

To You

Verily, verily, I say unto you,
Except a corn of wheat fall into the ground and die, it abideth alone:
but if it die, it bringeth forth much fruit.

John 12:24, KJV

...and that feeling, that feeling of being accepted back again and again,
of someone's affection for you expanding to encompass
whatever new flawed thing had just manifested in you,
that was the deepest, dearest thing he'd ever—

—George Saunders, "Tenth of December"

Table of Contents

Foreword

To enter these poems is to stumble onto a journey.

Our guide is the Beloved Wanderer, the narrator of the collection. The path does not promise safety. No one comes through this journey unchanged. That is exactly the point. Here, we become un-blinded to the world's wonders, we face the unraveling of self that is death, and we overhear unspeakable glory—the monstrously beautiful noise of all things becoming themselves.

Bower Lodge presents us a world thick with symbol. It draws from scripture, mythology, literature, and history, but also offers its own images: bold, sometimes tender, and frequently surprising. Given time, the book becomes its own map of interconnected stages on the journey. Threads of images emerge into woven themes: light as dangerous (and good), life as a dance of eating and being eaten, naming as a key to unlocking identity, descent as a path to transformation.

An ache of hunger and hope pulsates throughout, wild and ravenous. Though we might miss him, Christ also surely lurks here, hidden. Among other places, we catch him in the spider backlit against the kitchen window, the bone with gold marrow hammered open by a crowd, "the face that is mosaic, the face that is impossible and true."

The book's three sections correspond, respectively, to Good Friday, Holy Saturday, and Easter Sunday, and nods to resurrection punctuate the journey. In *Bower Lodge*, we learn that resurrection is more than a body passed through death to life; it is the final, holy re-integration of the fragmented self.

To read these poems requires—and accomplishes—an untethering. Only in the severing of umbilical cord can an infant's journey into this world be complete. Likewise, only in detaching ourselves from the need for a tidy understanding of ultimate things can we enter and engage their realm—and know the places where they touch us.

So, let us embark on this journey with a soulful curiosity, a curiosity that promises a bright return for our wonder. A curiosity that makes room for the strangely beautiful designs which unfold among our living, our dying, our transformations, and our redemption. Let us wander toward the *Bower Lodge*.

Abigail Carroll

Author of *Habitation of Wonder*, and *A Gathering of Larks: Letters to Francis from a Modern-Day Pilgrim* and Pastor of Arts & Spiritual Formation, Church at the Well, Burlington, Vermont.

And So Under

You are not only what is seen.
You are like what happens when
a desert shifted in a lost land,
like a pyramid long swallowed
by fine sand. Yes. A wanderer
comes, finds your utmost tip
(bleached like a horse tooth),
kicks you gently, thinks *weird rock,*
walks off, whistling. But
underfoot

         you lie entire.
Walls preserved by darkness,
chambers opening on chambers,
passages on passages (painted
with the tales you imagined
as a child), your cunning slits
aligned with summer stars
all raised up on the high, far day
that you were made, each awaiting
the earth's deep wind, the uncovering that
will reveal, reclaim, remember
the festival of your forgotten name,
the restoration of your unremembered crown.

One,

being words
written as the beloved Wanderer
sought the unwelcome sleep of Bower Lodge,
hand in hand with a lovely and implacable Embalmer,
who ruffled her long cloak
like the feathers of a brown bird,
toward that dread place set like death
in the heart of the river.

Leatherfoot

Two options: one
to go always in shoes,
buying and buying them,
wearing and wearing them
out, hurting less,
knowing less, being
shod   *nor can foot feel*

          or
be your own shoon, so
to say. I mean, let callous pack
and marble lushly. Brown
with your color and the earth's,
go on gravels or on carpets just so,
nervy, curling. Cold some, split
some, whorled and knotted, but
with ten toes feeling, leaving
prints no other leaves,
unsafe, unnumb.

Matthew 16:3

Nine minutes before,
I said if wind blew south
it would rain. Wind
blew south. Rain.
                    From
creek the cheers of ribald
frogs, who also have
their prophets.

Mill Pond

An even mile round the rim, slit with
sluices, locks, and flumes, each notch unaccountable,

tippling down abandoned water. The
mill's rough husks shadow and brown

the rushes, lay leaning angles, cement temples tuned
to unfashionable constellations. It is the granted

things we cannot comprehend. The child on a mountain
cannot see the mountain. Now, over this whole scene lay

the old photograph; see the mill regain its roofline,
over lanky men who stood in denim on the bobbing logs, rolled

cinematically with peaveys, laughed when greenhorns
wet their heavy boots, or better, thumped their nuts

against the trunks of a common, horizontal forest. In flannel hats the men
plump the sluices, leap locks, jumble on the flumes, shaking with the hungers

of an adolescent nation, lovely and offensive in their pimpled
industry, walking lolling water, stepped log to infinite hopped log.

More board feet passed through here than any other pond in America,
or so Bill Yeo coughs from a frayed lawn chair. Fine. Now, silent

as regrowing forests, the pond waits. What sinks will float. Affection.
Children on the mountain cannot see the mountain. Granted.

Touching the Horizon

Until we name, we stay unnamed;
until we give, we are ungiven.

Count your answers hard and green? Let them
ripen. You may have spent your life
evading the question. There will be time
to knuckle the wall of the sky.

Severed Lees

Live as if your life is true.
Time will come to know

what tangs mellow
in your heart's dry cellar.

Most of us are lying
with our days. See,

names do no good
until we tire of dissembling;

pop corks; pour severed lees;
serve the pressed, lost hours

we can't speak but which are saved
and someday may be tasted.

Missal

Hello

        dear friend. I saw you
standing by the pear tree
and tried to say hello. But
you moved away. Always half
an orchard before me, stride
for stride, quick and free among
the blossoms. A letter is a poor thing
compared to grasping your hands,
to kissing you. But you looked so well,
and how happy I was to
                  remember.
Time is a liquid that levels itself,
takes the shape of what it fills.
All streams run. Who can tie the water?
Seeing you brought back so many things
I thought were in the sea.
Will you visit? When the fruit is ripe
the branches bend. You do not need
a ladder. Will you eat a few?
Will you let me catch you
in the pale orchard or
the riverbed's long,
unforgettable avenue?

Hold

Hold your chest open—
let the dreams come through.

This one's a hummingbird
made of black rock.

This one's the ring
you found in a graveyard.

This one's a small god
worshipped with whiskey.

This one's a marble
as a child's glass eye.

This one's a birdhouse
I made from a gourd.

This one's the game of chicken
you play in the mirror.

This one's a pen
that makes words disappear.

This one's your grandmother's
preserved braid.

This one's the tuned crystal
in the center of a river stone.

This one's a horselord lying
on a picnic table in a field of tulips.

This one's your lost twin,
kissing you, asking,
*Do you think I or you
the stranger of the pair?*

Nine Kinds of Blindness

1. The one where your eyes do not work to see anything.
2. The one where your eyes do not work to see everything.
3. The one where your eyes work, but you cannot see what you have never seen before.
4. The one where your eyes work, but you cannot see what is inconvenient.
5. The one where your eyes work, but someone is keeping you from using them.
6. The one where your eyes work, but you are angry.
7. The one where your eyes work, but you are afraid.
8. The one where your eyes work, but there is no light.
9. The one where your eyes work, but there is nothing but light.

Mother, May I?

Walk the avenues of moss
where lichen trumpets, where finches spy
on sourgrass? Mother, may I find
the sparrowhawk's broad perch,
pick at owl pellets sopped in dew?

May I flick duff from heady toadstools
born in moonlight, surely not here
yesterday? Mother may I pluck
the red carnelian from the path,
carry it forever in my coat?

May I note the burling woods
where maples snapped in windy night
like pencils? Mother, may I
count the rings, know how old they were
when I was not, was small, was then?

Please, may I go all windy like the finches
where beauty wets her beak and coughs
a bone? Mother, may I
seek the hiding, find the blind
this arrow in my side came flying from?

The Sea, the Tower

The sea is not full
though she drinks every river.

The sand that rings the sea
was bone once, teeth, and jewels.

That sound you hear
is mountains falling, ground by time,

which must crash upon us also,
eroding like water,

which (the Magyar said)
will be the death of you

and which, if you could read
the waves, you would know in fullness—

for the card you drew last night
was the Tower.

Now, you wonder,
must catastrophe always be unpleasant?

Does sand struggle as it shrinks?
Do waves weep as they die on the shore

with laughter, with the wine-dark hymns?

After the Fires of 2020

To be read responsively by half-verse.

And in that smoke
>there is much of the body of a young boy

And in that smoke
>there is the useless embrace of his grandmother and all her hair

And in that smoke
>there are summer blackberries

And in that smoke
>there are voices saying it will be ok when it will not be ok

And in that smoke
>there are eight dozen doves within their cote

And in that smoke,
>there are cartons of cigarettes dropped on green linoleum

And in that smoke
>there are beaver dens and several factories

And in that smoke
>there flies a spirit with a red bullwhip

And in that smoke
>there are trees with black trunks and green needles

And in that smoke
>there are many tears

And in that smoke

there are the breaths of neighbors, gaunt like deer,
loping toward water,
toward low-mown fields that lie
far from the treeline

Good Friday

I see a man lay his arm open
with a short knife. Garlic is watered.
A laundress weeps, knowing she must wring
our clothes between her bleached ribs.
A child who has never wandered finds himself
suddenly alone, whimpers down the long hall.
A well that feels every drinker's lips as agony,
chooses still to flow. A bone with golden marrow is
hammered open by a crowd. They mock the
perfect treasure. An iron spring is pressed
into the ground, shuddering. I believe it
might propel this earth
beyond that darkening sun.

Question

When did you
last stop upon
the stair and
listen for the
voice in the
walls that has
been saying your
name for as
long as you
can remember, over
and over and
over again, with
heavy joy in
every syllable, that
you have done
your best to
explain to your
dear friends completely
without success because
to them it
sounds menacing, fearful,
but to you

there is a
blue beauty like
an iridescent insect,
a magnetic pull
like the scent
of pear blossoms,
an awakened memory
of the moment
that will define
you, which will
come once only
and which you
will not know
until it has
long passed away?

From Shuttered Graves

I sometimes hear a funny noise and think
how there's a grief that makes us chuckle,
a loss that nuzzles like a dog, how some aches
brighten life, more like crocuses than frost.

Morning glories tendril brown iron. A bird
has nested in the mausoleum. I hear the mower,
smell clotted grass clumping between headstones.
A cloud. A mouse. A molehill heaves

an antique ring. The arbor vitae has grown tousled
and immense. The red shadow of the obelisk
stretches by the church, whose windows all
look open from down here. My teeth are sore.

My eyes have dirt in them. My chest forgets to breathe
if I do not remind it. Look, the ring fits.
What were the odds? I sometimes hear a funny noise.
Do you think weeds are only slandered flowers?

Ashes in the Sea

The felon mouths
of rivers

span bank to bank,
spreading over sand,

who trickles, ripples,
catches sun and fascinates

like the inward oyster,
ceramic moon, salt-filtered.

The river is not still.
You cannot hush it.

You cannot ask where it came from
or whose clan bore it.

It is perfect in forgetting,
innocent as a sleepwalker.

Speaking only with stones

set unblinking

as the eyes of God
or a potato,

as if,

as if to say,
Why look where I have found myself.

Suddenly on this shore,
suddenly full of bleached wood and gull feathers,

suddenly come to the dominion of a blessed mother
who roars, who never named me,

who ties the tides about my wrists
to make rain, to hang me laughing from the sky.

Pinnate

Feel the heft
of memory

and toss it
in the pool.

When the ripples
cease again,

add seven vials
of oil.

Light the sheen
with a dropped match,

and blur your eyes,
discerning shapes.

See your death
in the flames

and know the shape
of your peace

will come like a leaf
veined and seeking sun,

a death that feeds
the rooted life

in the secret kingdom.

Bee Tree

I nearly cut it down
twice. It is dead—
or was dead—but my saw was dull,
and I felt lazy.

Today I sat back
in a chair beside the woods
and saw them.

High, twenty feet up perhaps,
like a droning school
of fish,

tiny, golden in the sun,
one by one,
one by one,
in and out,
in and out
and in.

The Son of Janus Dreams of Janus

I was a green shoot in summer,
late to the growing. But it was a warm autumn.
Sun looped sleek against a long sky,
and I split myself like first twinned sprouts
of waking seeds, leapt,

                       a sapling of the sky-high tree.
Now winter whispers like pressing cloves in apples.
Sleep is good. Stars tilt far faces to my dream
and cry a little. I shuffle husks of warm glad days,
memorize the canopy of trees, blue shadows etched
by moonlight, averaging to leaves.
                       In this life,
doors are much like dreams. We can walk
both ways. They can close. Sometimes
we must knock.

The Potato Diggers

Turned up a skull
with buds curling
in the eye sockets.

They rolled it
with a spade,
uncomprehending,
until the jaw
fell off.

Then, one fainted.
One ran to ring the cops.
One left yawning to dig elsewhere.
And one looked at me, accusing,
for he knew he was in a scene
of someone's making, and
no matter what he did,
it would become a symbol.

The Roof Slants,
So the Water Pours This Way

Do you think the world
might share a common, secret grief
for which we have no words—
as if each patch of lichen, every dog,
and even the black cormorants
who roll their long dives
all know the bald ache
we swallow?

Do we all go
from same evenings to
same mornings? Sleepwalkers.
Sighing drunks. As if we'll know the face
to rouse us only as it passes,
stalking back to where this started—
we apes with steeple fingers,
we who pray in roe and semen,
we composers of the bone-hymn
by those little swirling tidepools
on the coast?

Joy (Chemical Wedding)

For the French boy, it was a madeleine
in tea, which held the yearning
of a whole life: a curving path which runs
in only one direction, the press of time,
that slow bayonet. Memory distills
into the male

                and female principles.
Swan. Raven. A pen is set beside a cup,
mound of Venus, twitch of Mars,
brood of lordly Saturn flowing out
his paunch, the sacred pool and
the man of green hair who lives
beneath its water.

                    I smell a little gasoline
spilled on trimmed grass, and
the flush returns, a quick divide
to salts and essences, watching everything
that holds itself within itself, alternating futures
locked in a single glance, a path of swans
a child walks, tea and saucers, green eyes
for the magician's hidden golem, *ein sof,*
one fixed point at the center
of the world, the aleph, graal, the rosy cross,
joy itself,

                    a gleaming bayonet latched firm, which
barely breaks the skin
below my heart.

Her Dusking Avenues

If you cannot see
this city as expansive as a hive
or a nest of nursing rattlesnakes,
lightning balls, galls fallen from
hornets dancing in the broad oak
of the world; if

you are insensible to how
her dusking avenues mimic termite mounds and
the warrens of lean hares and
cliffside colonies of puffins; if

you don't see the shadow of the kelp beds
stretching over these buildings or
catch the sunlight through the carbon breath
as if filtered through twenty meters of saltwater or
note how the skyline drips upward like the lush stalagmites
in a caverned limestone hush,

then I do not think you will see much
when you walk this heavy earth
or listen if you're honored
with some revelation.

To the one with much, more.
But the one who lacks
will even lose his eyes.

Sky for Miles

The Fish of Heaven swam to me
and flipped his tail. Raw-boned,
fleshed with contentment, scaled with
notes from God's own whistling
in the shower. And the Fish said,
Why the long jaw? and I was like,
"You must've just got here."

                            He hung
lazy in the current of the breeze until
I added, "Look around. I am in love, but
my heart is not laughing. I sleep in
little dribbles. Nothing tastes the same.
The stars used to bloom like tulips. I thought
once I could grow to multitudes. I have
bad breath. I am either a happy ape
or a sad angel. Things die. I may be
losing my marbles. My tooth broke.
Then I swallowed it. I can't keep
the counters clean. There are men
with rifles everywhere. The fence posts
are rotten. I think every week how glad
I am my grandfather doesn't have to see this."

If that is all, he said,

                        then when
do you think you'll get around
to catching me?

Mothworm

I am the larva of an unknown moth.
I inch my way through to the inevitable shroud.
I daydream.
My cocoon shall be wound tight
and sink in my soft sides.
I shall become a soup of myself.
I curl about this branch.
I stretch several sets of forelegs in the air.
My rearlegs grip.
I form an inverted question mark.
I wave.
What question might I mark?
I sway, mimicking a chewed leaf.
I am the larva of an unknown moth.

Basement Caviar

Downstairs, you found a relative of whom
we do not speak. He has never shaved,
lives in the root cellar where mice crawl in,
where bare earth makes walls sweat. When
you met him, he invited you to fish.
Handed you a rod, whose line led down
through the floor into the filled-in well,
its bobber a blinking orange light bulb,
hook wired on below, some jagged ferrous metal
that spun your compass. It was not so bad
until he brushed the hair from his eyes.
You were afraid, ran upstairs,

                          but

every couple years, you've creaked back
down. You see him sitting in the halfway
flicker from the hole in that old ground,
eating richly from piles of black caviar.
He laughs. *Down goes up. You're missing out,
young one.* The rod bends underground,
as he pulls for his strange catch, stripping
line off the reel into the soil, buzzing,
singing pure joy as he hauls
the impossible fish.

Hourglass

The feeling is of sand behind
your eyes. There is no reason why
until you remember you've forgotten
your great grief again up in front
of your brain, but the core of you
is dry, is crystal circuit ticking like
a watch. The sand flows out the base
of your skull now. There is no reason why
you feel your belly fill

                        like a bag.
You stop being hungry for a while.
People look sidelong at a livid scar
you cannot find. Your teeth click
like a watch, grind like peach pits
dried on the counter. There is no
reason why. You inspect your molars
in the mirror. You think one has grown
a horrid little face.

                    A little time has passed.
You wish to cry, but the thing that weeps
needs sand to eat, and it all has flowed away.
There is no reason why until a hand
grips your narrow waist, flips you hissing
like a monk in penance, about to see
a revelation. Flips you, *shush*ing, praising
the light on the long water, flips you
to stand upon your head.

The Green Chapel
(Bower Lodge, Seen from Dry Ground)

Of course I knew that it would be a tomb,
old past memory, set in earth like
the socket of my eye sits in my skull,
that sloping ramp of molded earth,
that air that smells like undersides of stones—

knew that I would find it
giving root to moss and grasses, as I have seen
the sides of mausoleums, riven by artillery,
spill their midways corpses, who are becoming bones,
just skeletons of yellow-white and green—

still dressed, who still possess their hair. I think too
that I knew that such a place would repel me at the heart
even while it drew me by the guts,
that in its cool confine I would find my doom
and know if it was good or foul—

for when I was one year younger and a day,
I held the heavy axe and brought it down,
and in the final moment as skin and sinew tore,
I heard a voice I knew:
Welcome friend. It's only you you're striking.

Bower Lodge

You'll know the day has come
because you fear it.
The comfortable omens fail.
The geese fly north in winter.

Then will be the time
to do your first great dying,
to follow your familiar stranger
into the house you dread.

Set below the river
that cares not if you love it
but flows away regardless,
never twice the same—

a little like your soul,
this water that goes onward,
elegant and simple,
only what it is

and nothing more are you
laid down within the bower.
Here the lodge of death
smells of smoke and salt,

for the work of death is dying.
Not many of us do it.
We certainly expire,
but death is not the same

as expiration. It is
a clarity of being,
a last enunciation
that starts again anew.

So listen—die well
in the bower of the river.
Let it wash you of yourself;
then treasure what is left.

Your gift will be the greater
when geese fly south in summer.
You can call them to the river,
for you will know your name.

Bone Seed

Click crack
marrow sap
scrape clack
elemental bone seed,

plant me
arm deep
dry rot
gonna be a man tree,

in ground
root bound
no sound
wanna be a joy seed,

up now
skull town
bone sound
blooming like the true me,

click crack
blood sap
joint back
man tree from a bone seed.

Two,

an assembly of poems
culled from the multiform dreams
that poured like little bees
from the throat of the beloved Wanderer
as he lay mum among canopic jars, each
capped with his own head, holding safe each
precious disassemblement. The
Embalmer hums a tune stuck in her head.
There is honey in the lion,
stew bubbles up the cheery hive. See?
The holy sleep
of Bower Lodge.

The Pendulum

I held a shell on the beach.
Mussel nacre, Neptune's purple
lacquer, smooth as teeth. So
let it be written. The hermit's son
shall be a hedonist, the hedonist's boy
a hermit. You're living someone's
unlivable life. Small fits into big;
thin hunts the hollow of wide. How
do you name this—captivity
or freedom? So let it be done. I
lick the shell, give a yip. Tastes
like home: a blessed, mobile prison.

The Raspberry Kid

When you were a child,
you could take your mind
and throw it into all sorts
of things. One example:
you could expand until
you were the sun (that star
that sings the plasma operetta)
and focus yourself to a shaft
of particles, whose every move
remembered the first dance,
and fall to earth

               like the longest arrow,
flash past satellites, stratospheric lumination,
bounce the crystals of a cloud (which held vast tons
of water-weight, yet somehow sailed the air),
then take your sunset summer light, hot
with the vacuum dryness that ripens galaxies,
and without effort, without pain, stream back
eastward, compact yourself, romp the endless
cathedral of a raspberry, parade sacredly
the narthex of her red druples.

          Enter,
climb the altar, drink the holy cup,
preach a homily of all good things,
preach how to know this hidden kingdom
of plasma, marrow, rum, all below
must now turn lightward, heatward,
like twice-born little children.

The Mustness

Heir of life, a broad affection
is your birthright. A compass scribing all
which furthers self in self, which does not sign
lowliness by stature or by form, but knows those
signatures which elegantly drum the core of things.
Cherish the tempos of our rumpusing. Love:
the heirloom so obvious it may be quite forgotten,
like the joy of summer wasps, like your last name,
like outraged mint among the clover, like the dawdling
children of the twilight, like green berries, like dull blades,
like the story scars and smiles tell, like the canny danger
each life holds merely by becoming.

When I Think Upon the Seams

When I think upon the seams of gardens
pursing loam like lips finding first language,
I think how each tree's life sits not in leaf or branch
but right down low, where trunk peeps from the earth

and how my daughter saw for herself this fact. I think
upon my current clumsiness. My heart of loam puckers pink lips
like an infant, unintelligible, with only laughs and screams,
like an infant who cannot even name his colors.

Vertebrate Grove

No one taught you how to play
or how to stretch and yawn when you awaken.
No one ever showed you where your shoulders
meet your neck. How much you have in common
with the cat, the ostrich chick, the loping elk, the whale.

But what is kinship in the mind of a fool?
Human being, you alone of all the earth
are capable of sin, of forgetting you are
housed in bones. Deserts grow. Forests birth
new forests. Seas eat polar ice and rise, rejoicing.
On Ararat, the barren ark loses its tarred spine
as snows blow in, as clouds pour over the mountain.

In the place where lesser gods chew jewels, Noah
clucks at Gilgamesh, knowing three days underwater
will not drown his ego. In the place your shoulders
meet your neck, human being, my dear relative,
you have lost your sense of feeling.

Holy Saturday

I hear his feet on the spear ladder
climb down the soil past roots
through bedrock. He'll descend
until there is no lower in the world,
until the dead speak to each other,
*Do not arouse my hope but does that fresh one
know his name?* Then, by artesian springs
that have never seen light, the man
will toss his head and laugh and summon
a pale horse. To ride then, beating caverns
like a drum, shaking patriarchs awake,
brushing maggots from lost armies,
tying up his hair to keep it catching
on his scythe.

              For here's a reaping day.
Here's the time to stack corn before
the rain. One day, so many to gather.
Tomorrow these will all be laid
across those slender shoulders
like a brother hoists his father's
younger children. This cold lover
will climb again to bring a holy day
to twilight eyes and holy dusk to those
blinded by the light.

Now falls the hour
to feel the bone beneath our skin.
Death shall peel our flesh from us, toss it
to the dogs of time. But listen as you wither
to his feet upon the spears. We in darkness
have seen great light. None shall be spared
the lovely, vicious day borne up, restless in the grass,
rising. None shall sleep through this shout
from our buried Conqueror.

Right Angles

We leave the simple things
alone and unconsidered:
the plumage of a moth,
the fact that trees must measure
right angles to the earth's dear core.

We who live in wonders
must be blind to wonders.
If fish could see the water,
they could see nothing else.

The light must break here slowly
lest every eye be seared,
lest we all be magicians
measuring the world,
geometers, tall fainters in the light
tracing in mathematics
the single mystic ecstasy.

On Prayer, Like a Forest
Making Weather

I, with my halfways piety,
the tilted prayers
that wobble in my mouth,
who praises like I drink—
too often to be quite respectable,
too little to know quite what I am doing,
I have shuffled to the woods,
whose fog streams up in unrepentant mornings,
up to teach itself, to learn how to join
its little newness to the everlasting clouds.

The Tearing of the Green

The acorn soaks
in warm soil,

swells
to twice
its former size.

No one
who walks above
hears it groan.

No one
hears the slow
split crack.

No one
sees the shell
blacken.

No one
sees the seed
eat itself.

We only see
the sprout.

We only see
the child of the oak.

Birdsap

The alder's failing now
and breaks heavy
with the rain.

The bark folds
like the coat of a man
who knows he'll no more need it.

About its roots,
fungus trumpets, reveling already
(orange and red, orange and red)

in shelves and tiers
and rondy cups
like cauliflower ears.

The flicker comes
with black upon the throat
to eat what plays below the bark—

yellow things, tan things,
writhing black heads
and bellies that pop,

flailing things, half-made things
who have no armor,
whose mandibles protest, *not yet, not yet*—

and in the flicker's craw,
the flesh of grubs is taken, loved,
and made into a paste.

This rises like dough,
is ground, digested.
It is clarified like butter.

When whole and pure,
it flows into the genitals,
and poured into a little shell.

So it is no coincidence
that egg yolks shine like suns,
for birdsap is the summer light

from years ago
when the alder was ferocious
and impregnable.

When it stood
against the coming of the winter,
every leaf attentive

to its light,
before the fungus
(red and orange, red and orange)

and before the flicker
with the black throat
and the multiform, infinite call, I wonder—

when the alder slurped the earth,
did it dream it would become
a yellow glow suspended in an egg?

The Ash Breeze

Tanagers are pairing in the hazel stand
to twitch on errands to the fir line,
then to alders who wet their feet
along the windy lake. The males are bright
as dahlias. Their mates are brown and dusky
like fircones if fircones grew black eyes
and fell upwards.

            It is a peaceable truce
I've found with myself, watching tanagers
pairing in the hazel stand. A moment to rest
in these doldrums on the life-map, when
("becalmed," the worst word for a windless
agitation) you and I bend at our oars. "Time
to ride," you say, "the ash breeze," and
here we are again, I guess, within the blue horizon
where water falls to sky, where no wind moves,
save that for which we pull. This is the latitude
of sloshing prayers, where horses panic in the hold
and dream of drowning in the sunken stables,
where skeletons prance free of heavy skins to graze
among the coral.

"Oars are wings now," I say,
back from my daydream of tanagers, back
where I cannot tell if we are moving as we bob
and pull against the world's salt tears. As
hoofbeats ring on boards below. As
we learn no sailor knows his weight
until he's had to row it.

How Still

The
tumbling rock slide
comes to rest

like
shattered temples
against level ground

whose
soil still
hides unbroken monuments,

fills
earthen gaps
with headlong silences,

dripping
like dreams
down raggy dirt,

so dark
and blind
like worms
whose tales
of light
come fearfully
as myths:

Up there,
            they say,
the bright star
falls to crush you.

Yonder Lies the Hawk

Beneath the window
(in New York all is windows)

underdown against the sidewalk
beside black plastic bags

head cocked back
as if in adoration,

as if tracking a high star
and dreaming

how it would feel
to plunge up

through the ethers
into the second heaven,

how it would feel
to hunt some younger god

among the fields
where the black roars

weightless, rakish feathers,
a cry of stark command,

the killing reach,
the claws that sheath in flesh,

how it would feel
to earn one's constellation,

to be named by some far mind,
The Hawk,

to feast on fire
and gushing heavenly gases

to breathe once more forever
in the spacious place

instead of lying
with a broken neck

beneath this window
(in New York all is windows),

instead of finding out
that one was striking oneself

in the placid and infinite mirrors.

The Snags

Old lures hung by winter flood tangle
tilted alders. From the brown pool,
trout watch them spin: puckered spoons
delicately strung, monofilamental, ornamented;
pink and vicious fuzz; treble hooks; rooster tails;
imitation frogs whose limbs thump bass
challenges to those who hunger in the speckled water,
who swim oblique in sundry variegations, aching to rise
for bright painted things, the impossible fruit of the alder,
neon tidbits of eternal beauty.

Little fish, remember what hangs
bright beyond your reach, the knowledge
that would pierce you with its horrid loveliness,
pull you, thrilled, protesting, gooped and bloody at the gills,
into the air.

Thorn of My Thorn

Thorn of my thorn, branch of my branch,
what brought you to the river
and the lodge of the embalmer?

I pruned the plum so poorly in my youth.
My shears were sharp, I grant you,
but a boy's mind was behind them.

Still, blossoms found their way
down branches, still
buds burst, still
leaves harkened, still
roots rooted until summer heaved,
and every open flower
was an eye.

Now I have set my heart aside,
set my liver and my brain aside,
set my entrails and my stomach aside
in jars of salt, jars held by hands
I know too well to fear.

And I shall take them up again,

when I unwind myself
within the lodge. I shall put them
to the use of one who now has rested
and can live. I shall test
the promise that a man
can cleave in love
even to his prunings.

Temple Day

I saw Earth stretched cayenne-colored,
shivering with frost, chrome-like. She
wore palm fronds embroidered on her skirts, as if
her bells were fruit like pomegranates, as if
her pomegranates rang as scarlet bells. And
cherubs flew, whose wings of endless eyes
flapped querily, million vermillion pupils focusing,
unfocusing in pleasure, whose wheels turned lusciously
in wheels, whose sides veered off in non-Euclidean
angles, who each seemed perched

                                        forever on the edge
of eternal, glorious death by immolation. Flames were
plumes to them. They preened feathers of unbeing
while God pulled from their breasts a dozen bushels
of tiny hearts like pomegranate seeds, each beating
only once, a little chime that shook down several stars.
I watched the delicate lacing of Earth's brown fingers
with unspeakable wingbones, with the throne-bird-chariot-cloud
that held the awesome train, bending beneath him who sat
on them (though they were the ones upheld) until
they folded like the shell-shape of a walnut,
mimicking the brain within my skull.

               Then, a choral shriek—
the sacrifice caught blaze, love lapped water from the trenches,
the bullock kissed the eagle, the lioness curled about the man
until they shared my face, the cayenne-chrome bloomed scarlet
in my fingers, and I saw above it all to the face that is mosaic,
the face that is impossible and true.

To an Arch Enemy

If you let me see you, let me
love a small thing that you love, honor me
with your woeful and most purple
mourning, I believe our gulfs will shrink,
that we can just stretch to touch
a good thing which the other touches, that
I and you will find we both support the keystone,
just straining, as we inevitably must,
in opposite directions, holding, together,
the arch.

A Leaping Salmon,
Falling Back to Water

Here I have flown
in what cannot hold me.

My breath is held;
my breath will hold me.

My dry eyes gaze on holy things
which line the river with a blur.

My breath is not held;
my breath will not hold me.

I will whisper of this to the eggs
when they are laid, and milt
      is spilled over their gravel,
when crayfish worship gods of death,
when water snakes spell dreams above me,
when languidly the current heaves
      the little stones against the little stones,
when eddies darken with the fallen leaves.

My breath holds me;
my breath will never hold me.

Three,

*being poems written
after the beloved Wanderer
waked again beside his Embalmer in the river
and rose from the death-silk to stumble
in slow, concentric circles (gradually widening)
before walking on his way
enlarged with seeing wings:
the gift of Bower Lodge.*

The Yearning

Joy does not spare us easily.
In Montavilla, I had this neighbor
who kept a teenage tortoise. It weighed
ninety pounds, was named Buddha or
something like Buddha. One April, a
crowd gathered while he mumbled down
a burm, tore dandelions from their
steepnesses, chewed like he knew he'd
outlive America.

                 Buddha could not be
lifted. To move him: a trail
of lettuce and bright vegetables curved
twice round his unmown demesne, up
a wheelchair ramp, back in the
house. Longing was his leash. One
does not own such a one.
His jog took hours or decades;
joy does not spare us easily.

The Old Bay

Come, let there be a sun
over the arch of the boats: a green sun
for a change, a light in which
the pale stones may be lifted up, in which
the little stones may be lifted up, in which
the hard eyes of the grandfathers can soften
as they search over the bows
for their several reflections.

Calving

Calving: when a glacier sloughs
a vast and precious portion, pays
water's loan.

                Birds rise. Ice of Eden
bobs the glass-green brine pitching fits,
yawing yawned lessenings. Weight below the
waterline tips always southward. The last
mammoth slumped on an arctic island
circa 2000 BC. Yes, when kings licked
fresh paint in Knossos. One world knelt
shaggy to a stone beach, a second leapt
the sun. Lithe like a youth gone vaulting
the immortal collects, our Minoan bulls.
We become our metaphors. Calving.

Joy, Which I Once Called a Bayonet

Is sharpened by omissions. Last year, I
walked out back to this one spot
where indigo squirrels pong
between green walnuts
and black woods. There
is a stone wall. There
is a yellow creek that wets the boulders. There
are denim darks of fir-shadow, which should
drown seedlings, but also there
in impossible cracks, lost hollows,
and God's unaccountable brown logics,
grow the plantings: a dozen little nut-trees,
each with a copper name, a treasure coiling oily roots,
which lived by being lost,
which live, which dawn and
golden with good sheens, which dream of
seeds to plump like wrinkled brains, which likely
pray that each young ball will fall to fates like theirs,
quite happily misplaced. The squirrels
pinged everywhere, burying.

Bearing Witness

Ask no secrets of the humming heart,
whose slender tongue dips flowers
for their sugar. Rather, lay your ear
to the foot's thick heel. It colors itself
with roads; it has the knowledge.

Gone to Ground

"...there is silence, without complaint."
Wallace Fowlie, on the work of Robert Bly

I went to ground and lost my edge.
Like a hare to his hole and lost my edge.
An axe chopping earth, I lost my edge.
A knife cutting stones, I lost my edge.

The mail piled and tipped; I lost my edge.
People asked where I was, but I'd lost my edge.
I got puzzled stares. I lost my edge.
The phone stopped ringing. I lost my edge.

I thought before I spoke—lost my edge.
Dreamed slow useless things and lost my edge.
Became stories, not sermons. I lost my edge.
Knew arrows and buttercups. Lost my edge.

But I saw with both eyes, for I'd lost my edge.
I felt with both hands. I lost my edge.
I went joying and crying. I lost my edge.
My hair grew with vines. I lost my edge.

Now a great fool am I. (Lost my edge.)
Living under the cliffs, for I lost my edge.
I'm all gone to ground. I lost my edge.
But never have I cut sharper.

The Heron Pecks a Banded Agate

Live in your body;
do not talk of pyramids
if you don't know your hands.

Feel how the grain
of this table
is the story of a tree?

Have you forgotten
you hold your
every day within you?

Nostalgia

Has there ever been a man
who felt suited to the time
for which he was born? No,
I think something in the psyche trips a wire
about the summer you become yourself,
and the little popgun that is triggered
goes *thbob* right at your heart
and drops a little flag—

　"bang"

and you find yourself like Jonah,
praising the fish that ate you
because always looking backwards spares you
from the great work of your life.

Kintsugi Song

For Makoto

Glinting, I chant the space between
what ought to touch:

               honor all
snapped threads, gild knees with
callouses. I chant fragments of a
priceless bowl swe

            pt on tiles by a broom—I
chant slips and irreversible disasters, wiltings,
failures, scars, the little disappointments
and the large, blue streaks down a
world that wishes it was only
suncolors. I chant upended sight,
name precious every jagged
everything; I brush compassion like
urushi. I chant wrinkles,
heartaches, lamentations for the
lively dead, undustings
of the dust, unbreakings
of the br

        eaks. I chant gold
into the cracks. Touch my
roughness, my smoothness; if such

honor is not faith,
then what could make peace, what
mend a heart with double-blessed and
most offensive
beauty?

Broken Mystic Virgin Song

When time has ceased and all her labored points still into one,
when centuries and hours linger each as long,
when the evenings and the mornings stop together on the stairs,
then I'll love you, and you will not be alone.

Where to a vicious edge the dull infinities converge,
where space suns his belly like a cat and yawns,
where the bounding soil knows itself a better name,
there I'll know you there you and I will be as one.

But now and here the oil in the crescent lamps must burn
and spew their little light. Here and now dark friends must wait
and wonder if the Bridegroom has forgotten, and
in turbulence of windy time and space, the hyssop and the turtledove
blanch pale beneath the eyes of long unblinking streets,
beneath a clock that does not strike and ticks on without hands.

Oh, Heart Beholding

Oh, heart beholding
yourself in vain,
the heartheath, the wasted place
where spirit knocks ribs
like a loose-rattled house shutter,
heard the news?
The light of cities is near.
The light of cities is hungering.

Oh, heart becoming
yourself in vain,
smoky heat hearth, fire wastrel grace,
when the rattle-loose rib shudder hurts you,
do you heed the news darkly?
The killer of cities has seen you,
electric, unyielding.

Hey heart, can you hear me?
First fists, first fruits,
fruits, fist-sized, trellis up ribs
to rattle and ripen. One per spirit.
Oh heart belonging,
they wait the beating basket
of the light unyielding,
light of cities, happy
heart hunting lengthening
hunger of God.

Ephesus at Sunset

1.

Alkaline song in my acid mouth,
the Christ-hymn spills a dear free
going of words, of praise-barks
slung slobberwise, as if I am a dog
who's caught his master's scent:

      you came you came you came,
and I have gone all clumsy in the tongue,
gone flop, gone adolescent in my joy, every
limb tripping every other limb
because I see a star come over the horizon
just now, a star that speaks only its own name
then mine, each syllable a prism of ground glass,
slinging light, each syllable a humming crystal egg,
a snapping diode, an alkaline song.

2.

Then I was elbow-deep in dishwater.
I looked up as sunset light just caught
a spider on her window-web, as she
(backlit) tiptoed up her tightrope
to a sac of eggs just at the hatch, where
silhouetted like a shadow puppet
from the mahogany islands, she waved

her frontward legs, welcoming
her dear immortal young who spilled out
the worn and flattening bag, rejoicing, rejoicing,
　　　we came we came we came,
"And this," I thought (all soapy at the wrists),
"is a type, a revelation, this" (rinsing a chipped bowl)
"is Christ."

3.

In other ages this was not known,
and even now is quite forgotten (how few
words it takes to tell the Mystery),
but it is all here, all in this first love
from which we either fall
or trip upon, trip on upward,
all us eight-legged puppies come happy to the hatch,
to our first broad glimpse of Mother-master, that star in burning web,
that maiden-cry, that blossom and that slit,
that sword dragged sharp on sidewalk brick,
that soap froth shaken in a filthy cup,
that sunset for the world, which shall turn to
our last and backward dawn:
　　　become become become.

Kind Time

Love, our smiles
have been carved
in wrinkling apples,
growing kind like God is kind,
who gives so many gifts
they wither us.

Joy, Spilled Freely
From Love's Red Obelisk

If I ventured to confess my love, to say to you, my dear,
that nothing you might do would drive me from your side,
that I would fill the pit up with my blood for you
like St. Agnes's doomed suitor, I wonder if a fire kindled on my hand
would burn me half as hot, would maim me half as much.

For isn't love like ours a crippling thing?
Its leaping is the leaping of a slaughtered lamb;
its singing is the singing of a strangled fish
tossed high up on the sand, for whom the foreign element
is death, is twenty deaths, all gasping with broad ecstasy,

                        my God my God O why have you forsaken me?

But this is still the joy, the holy and divine appointment,
pressed hot into the hand all wonderful and bleak.
The monument in us was built for death and pleasure;
the stones of us were carved with letters for each other.
And when we are deciphered dear, do you not expect

our ancient languages to spell some prayer?
Perhaps we each are half the old red obelisk,
spilling ceaselessly the spurting joy of love
nourished in foundation by the sacrificial blood,
always all unknowable and always pointing home.

Ocean Park

I will go where sea is never still,
where sky seems wider than sun's sweep
and sawgrass sings, where brown birds curl
behind the wind, and fog rolls in, filling dunes
like smoke from the eternal battle, where
days leave souvenirs, gifts washed in my tidal mind,
where the long, dark song of me is sleek and winding—
so blithe that I can dream of walking
       straight from this shore
across the surface of the deep.

Hard By

Hard by my knowledge I have come
in tangled diode thought, in black
and yellow testing of the truth. The hill
that stands below the house of God
is difficult and causes stumbling. Far
from this mountain come our pilgrim
minds, all saffron-colored, teeth black
as vanilla pods.
                    Saints crack themselves
against this road, releasing savors
as they die, husks blown through mullein
in the ditch. Hard by my painful end
I've come, by honest lies, by new ropes
never used. And now the alabaster loom
from which my fabric rolls sounds like
a spool of bone, as Wisdom weaves a cloak
of me, of you perhaps, lain crossways on the warp
of hair, shorn, blood-dyed, woof made
from her traveling children.

Carnal Wonders

A turkey formed of amethyst,
which tinkles like a music box
when shot,

a salt cellar set in your left
forearm that fills anew each time
you weep,

a stain that spreads across
your face each time you wrong another
and lingers until rinsed,

a coat, wide enough to hold
all who call you friend
but that is your own hair,
woven and felted,

a tree with mouths for leaves,
each of them praising the sun
with a faultless shout.

Rodentia
(Song Remembered from a Dream)

O mouse
with purple eye
and broken yellow yardstick,

why do you come
all sad and measuring?

Why do you come
a little sick Napoleon?

why do you come
all draining like a wound,

when you could trot
a field of grass,
lost in joy?

What the Spider Said

Learn the arts of everywhere while nowhere;
weave willowed funnels for yourself;
stalk only what may be eaten;
become what swings between;
fish the air;
pull from your sanctuary the silverbridge;
spin prismatically with octagonal refractions;
know the good arithmetic but never count;
pray no one sees your beauty;
be largely soundless;
make peace with being largely soundless;
feed in silence;
don't bite what you can't bind;
wash your long legs in sunlight;
raise your mandibles in pure praise;
give thanks, give thanks, give thanks;
know graciously the crystalline and everlasting dews.

Missed Forever

You just missed forever.
It was here not long ago,
but you were so loud coming up the gravel.
Spooked it. Look—can you see
the impression it made in the soil where
it sat back on its haunches, threw its head back
and sang? Rustle in the grass. Perhaps it
dropped a feather or a pearl. You might
track it. It made for the west, and I expect
you'll catch it if you run. It cannot have
gone far. Or, as this is advantageous ground,
there is something to be said for waiting
to see it return. You will likely hear
it coming up the road before you see it.
And while you wait, why not crouch here
in the grass? Why not examine these pearls?
Why not throw back your head and sing?

The Choice

The choice is not between
right or wrong,
bright or dim,
good or evil.

It is not whether
to make alive or kill,
plant or uproot,
preserve or consume.

Neither must you choose
between truth and falsehood,
pain or comfort,
richness or poverty.

The choice is what
it has always been:
whether in the next moment
you will be yourself
or whether you will not.

Pillar

Put your palm just here, son—
the seam's where mortar's weak
and stone joints might be wobbled,
and think of how they tried to blind you
by spooning out your eyes. They could
never see why that might give you sight
beyond their reaching.
                              There is still
honey in the old bones. Behold, those
who dress fine live in kings' houses, but
our good work's down here, setting
shoulders to the pillar, pushing,
teaching them to step to heavy music.

Man-size

I then came to know myself
not as carver but as statue under mallet's arc,
half-face, loplumped, pushing from new
marble, who only gained his eyes when flakes fell
that had been his cheeks.

                      Whose brow
furrowed or relaxed as chisel chipped,
who gained features by subtraction
of what he thought he was. Yes.
My block used to be so much something
I was nothing, slab of rigid possibility,
stone that could not live until potential
had all been chunked away.

My Sons

My sons, this is a bitter time
when you have come of age. The crow
pulls foil from the earth. The rain
is mixed with ash. The ground
is hard to plow, yet we must turn the dirt.
The work is more than ever needed,
yet less help shall we get than any
of our fathers.
                        I address you
with a solemn charge: be courageous.
Do not despair. Do not fall prey
to the bleached liar who whispers
from the shoulder that this is not
our mess. I address you, and
all our fathers stand to agree.
I have seen their faces in the darkness
of my meditation, in dreams that carried
me like a horse, then bucked and left me
weeping.
                We charge you to be strong,
simple of heart, light in the stirrups,
gentle on the reins. Eager to the hunt,
quick to laugh, slow to bitterness.
Hard and merciless upon what you
must strike, full of compassion for all
things lovely.
                        Glory comes to those

who are present at the crisis. Win honor
for our name by your love and bravery.
You will bless this hour of long sadness. Then,
you will take your place in the quiet light
with those who brought you here, with
honor and esteem. Your ancestors will ask
to shake your hand, and ancient kings will smile
to list you in their lineage.
                              I shall be there.
It will be my joy to hold you again, to kiss you
on each cheek. It will be my joy to say,
Through these I served the world.
Through these I struck a blow
at wickedness and folly. Though the year was bleak
and all the omens foul, there was found a good thing in us
yet, life in the strange stock fate planted in the rebel dirt.
Life yet in the sons of the sky-high tree.

The Fly

Describes right angles to itself,
a knight in midnight blue,
iridescent armor flashing as he
climbs the square tower. Walls invisible,
steps invisible, no sallyport or
crenellations save a changeable breeze,
plays sentry to a siege
of time, of harrying valor
that carries scent of fruit,
of ferment on the wind,
promising victory hard won, puddles
of syrup sipped at dusk,
ten thousand armies of children
to defend, squirming like living
rice, calling out the praises
of the delicious dead, guarded
by their armored ancestor, joyous
maggots, dreaming below the tower
of the shy, ripening air.

A Wayward Scent and Strong

A wayward scent and strong, chemical,
like crushed ants, sweet as smell of sweat,
of which every form of language fails.

Here it comes again on breeze from fallow field
like clover mown and dry, like irises in sun.

Name it, I dare you, before the breeze shifts,
before the palate is cleaned by too much thought,
before we speak of it as a memory.

In Passing

The light
      is passing through.

The wind
      is passing through.

The life
      is passing through.

The fear
      is passing through.

The rage
      is passing through.

The dark
      is passing through.

The song
      is passing through.

The thought
      is passing through.

The dream is passing, too.

The ache,
the gall,
the seed,
the joy—
      these all are passing through.

Through you—
      and you are passing, too.

Hungry Things

All hungry things are robbers
of a grave. There is no eating
but the eating of another, no life
except what comes from lamenting,
long surrender. It is hypocrisy to look
away from maggots. There is a secret
place in each of us where dreams
are made. If you find it with your
daytime mind, fear will meet you there.

But make of fear a damp and honest
friend. Stay; do not close your eyes.
Take with honor the mirror she hands you;
trust you will know what to do when she
gives you forty-nine yarrow stalks and whispers,
                Throw them and divine.
You will kindle a dry, hot digestion, and
with the hope of God, who swims below
you in the earth and flies above
you in the heavens, you will see
your swollen belly holds a seed.

Apogee

The arc your heart cuts through the sky—
silver needle trailing threads of vapor.
Bright parabola, hissing mint, fizzing blue,
until last lost light of day flames rough
in red of hearty crisis, and clouds
catch like tinder;

                        through
that sudden-blazing wool, past fear,
past any expectation, the great
game's arch is made—shape of life,
length of soul, your only precious angle
seen whole, end to end, adding
your single atmospheric color to
the ringing, general glory.

Prophecy

In the last days, every particle
of sun will sing crucifixion.
Leaves of lost books
fluttering in wind
will flip and blur,
spelling the great name
whose trumpet tones:
Christ Jesus will roar
like burning wool,
like waterfalls that wear
stone hearts to grit
with everlasting
judgments and compassions—
and I say, for I have seen it,
that the wound in my left arm
will speak mysteries
as a small mouth;
that tears, bottled
by vintages and years
will come uncorked,
foaming golden, gushing
goblets for the wedding;

that all things shall become themselves
in the flowered, antecedent glory,
an unspeakable praise
that would be monstrous
if not perfect in its goodness
and kaleidoscopic beauty,
turning, arranging new geometries,
turning, clicking colors upon colors.

Bashō by the Saltshaker

I am in a diner. The table is that boomerang
formica we all know but has no name. Coffee here
never becomes cold. "The Law of Love"—I once
thought *law* meant *rule*, but now I see
it's *logic*. Magnetism. Gravity. Bleak innocence, a
self-consistent nature. The cherry must push blossoms,
cherishing its intricate extremities; crickets must sing
in helmets of dead soldiers. Curved wood,
once knowing wind, must impossibly return
to the empty, throwing hand. *I am who I am.* The
uncertain certainties. The Laws, the Loves.

Psalm

For God alone my soul in silence waits;

a snail who sleeps on undersides of leaves,
who bathes in rain that runs from foot to head,
whose lucky trail gleams silver down the grass,
whose pilgrimage makes anywhere a home;

for God I wait, for God I wait alone.

On a Country Porch, in May Rain

The rizz and raggle of my laden thought,
the feet that slink up sagely in the hedge,
the whistle and the thistling of the birdy ditch,
gone up and scattering; tires down the gravel bend.

Assignment

You will go now on your way
with all you need
in your empty hands.

The road will be
harder than you'd like,
and the water to ford
like glaciers.

On the plateau
you'll choose the pony
that speaks with her eyes
and ride until you have forgotten this letter,
forsaken every word
of your native language,
bled out every vein,
been replenished by new marrow,
and (like a cloud dark with rain)
remembered who you are.

Bower Nest (Resurrection)

This last I hesitate to tell. It is too near
my spirit. I cannot do it honor. But
as I lay on the embalmer's slab
in the death lodge, in the river,
it seemed to me my hut of sticks was sliced
by sunlight like a scalpel, and the great Star,
with surgeon's mask and gauze,
reached to take me like an infant
from my winding sheets.
                    And as he lifted me
from where my grubflesh length had crawled
to perish and wiped my face and gave me
a new name (I may not utter it), I looked below me
at the bower in the river. I saw that it had always been
the belly of a mother, a tomb that was a womb,
blooming like a rose of woven sticks, diligent,
feathered as a nest.

                    A bell,
a long-drowned beak, a secret bloomed in crystal,
a sunken holy incense tube, a skull,
a spiderweb, potato-eyed and yawning,
a walnut, the impossible fish, a mirror
that gave one's twin, little trails of berries in
the blessed water, a ladder leading down
that now I see leads up as well, right angels
all along it, pollen-covered, chorusing
like bees.

       Leads up past stars, past seven thunders
(whose faces blend the horse-look with the dog)
to the bleeding feet of one who has been all eaten,
and so may now rejoice, devouring all
in light, in blue-red siren light
and hornbald trumpet triumphs,
as
      with a little knife he peels a stick,
elegant and whipping as a willow,
as with his tawny hands
              he cracks a bough
and adds it to the pile by his side.

Benediction

Someday will come your knowing
that not all that can be done
must be done, that you were always free
to be who you were, that one only
and no one else. In that
blessing you will go, from and in it,
for and to it, blessing you
will go, and into the grass
of the long valley you will
go in peace.

Acknowledgments

Thanks are due to those early readers of this project (and individual poems in it), who offered various encouragements and sound counsels. Besides the other two members of The Garden Party (Abigail Carroll and Leslie Williams, whose substantive encouragement and edits were the stuff of sheer love), these readers included Emily Pastor, Ted and Bethany Rydmark, Alyssa Agee, Daniel Leonard, Raymond P. Hammond, Anthony Ashley (and that group of young Colorado men in the shed who shared some extremely precious discontinued Frog Morton tobacco and stamped and shouted at my first reading of "My Sons"), Adam MacInturf, Marly Youmans, Forrest Johnson, Justin Rigamonti, Kristopher Orr, D.S. Martin, and others.

Thanks to Jacob Cowdin, whose creative collaboration here has been pure joy. Jacob, you are a true artist and a good man.

Thanks to Eric Muhr at Fernwood Press for saying yes to this book, and to their whole team for bringing it into the world.

Thanks to a particular bend of Rock Creek in Vernonia, Oregon, that sits behind 348 C Street—a place that became more part of me than I knew.

Finally, eternal thanks to the Spirit of Life, whose ways are like the wind's ways, and whose every movement is wildness and love.

About Paul

Paul J. Pastor is a writer living beside the Columbia River in Oregon. His writings on spirituality blend a love of the Christian Scriptures with wide-ranging interests in literature, art, philosophy, and culture, and a unique intimacy with the natural world. His work has won numerous awards and critical recognition for its beauty and depth. His work crafts timeless images and ideas to speak boldly to the wounds and possibilities of our age. *Bower Lodge* is his first book of poetry.

Paul is the author of *The Face of the Deep* as well as his multi-volume poetic devotional, *The Listening Day*. With a M.A. in Biblical and Theological Studies from Western Seminary, Paul brings his passion to life as a speaker at churches, retreats, and universities. He presently serves two imprints of Penguin Random House, as editor, acquiring and developing new authors and books for their world-class publishing program.

On the Art of *Bower Lodge*

Transformation is the theme of Bower Lodge,
so it made sense to me that the artwork would also go through stages
of change (as does most of my artwork).

Each piece in the book was digitally drawn and colored,
then projected and traced by hand,
hand-carved into lino blocks, then finally hand-printed.
Each stage left its own unique mark on the artwork.

Coming out of a year of solitude, collaboration was front of
mind for me, so when we decided to hand-carve the inspired
imagery, it seemed only natural for Paul and I to do so together.
The two of us sat together for many evenings carving,
printing, talking, getting to know each other.
Becoming friends. Creating art.

I love the striking natural imagery we used,
each piece serene in its own way, connected to nature,
but clearly created by the human hand.
However, what I enjoy more is the memory and collaboration in creation.
It's one reason this series is so near and dear to me.

—Jacob Cowdin

Title Index

A

B

C

E

F

G

H

I

J

K

L

M

N

O

P

First Line Index

A

B

C

J

L

M

N

O

W

Y

Printed in the USA
CPSIA information can be obtained
at www.ICGtesting.com
LVHW050742240424
778285LV00002B/21